The Journey within me

Simran Sachdeva

BookLeaf Publishing

India | USA | UK

Presentation by *BookLeaf Publishing*

Web: www.bookleafpub.com

E-mail: info@bookleafpub.com

ISBN: 9789358315103

First edition 2023

Broken vase

Walking down a summer evening
In a green gown and shining heels
Your eyes glittered up when you first saw me

I looked back in your eyes
All I could see was a fire, passion and a hidden
sadness
Urge to be desired ,urge to be loved
Urge to be heard, urge to feel seen
I fell in love with the beautiful smile you had
I fell in love how you made me laugh
I fell in love with your ability to express every
emotion unfiltered
Suddenly in my journey of life
I had vision of a hand intervened with mine with
a promise of being there
From a stranger , you became my home
Your arms could treat my tiredness, my pain, my
sorrows
You weren't , but I made you that powerful
You were a broken vase and so was I
But we were different
As day and night
As Sky and land

As I came with my broken pieces to mend you
with my love
But you left when you felt complete
I stood there with the broken and missing pieces
of mine.
I'll be your broken vase now.
With time I will heal, I will complete myself
with love I will endure myself with
But you won't be able to forget me ever, because
remember you have my broken pieces
You are made with parts of me
So as I go as a broken vase now with no regrets
but love in my heart
You will live forever with my broken pieces and
love I poured in making you complete my love.

As I step everyday ahead without your forehead
kisses , I embark a journey to find my pieces
within me so I don't bleed on those who never
cut me.

Hope

She paused the song on her phone.
It was pin drop silence
Until she allowed herself to observe around

Standing on her terrace
She heard the rusted wheels of trains nearby
She heard the weathering leaves of trees
She heard the jamming car horns
She heard the wind, the rustling sound

She felt the breeze pass through her
It was like the moments before heavenly rain

She allowed her self to feel

She felt her childhood in the fragrance of wet
sand.

She felt peace when she looked at the sky with
hues of blue and white coloured clouds turning
grey.

She felt free when she saw the birds flying in the
sky with their open wide wings like they could
see the heaven.

As the sun rests to bed with the rising moon,
The city lights from there seems like stars on
earth.
As she admires every breath and smiles with
every breeze that passes by her.

With her eyes closed
She took a deep breath with her head towards
the dawn sky

And there it was, first drop of awaited rain
And in that very moment, she knew everything
will be okay.

My secret

5

Come close,
And I will tell you all my secrets
Come closer,
And I will make you my dirty little secret.

The Romantic Virgin

I remember that day as clear as crystal
It was the time of dawn in the start of spring
when he first touched my bare skin, kissed all
over my naked body with his soft lips
And I lost my title of a romantic virgin.
I recall it as it was the day I understood my
desires, my body and myself just a little more.
I had dream or moreover a vision of this perfect
way of experiencing that level of intimacy with
someone the first time and always wished for
someone with eyes on fire, passion and spark
when they look at me.
It's like the things you don't like about yourself
but then experiencing someone laying down
next to you with their naked body and burning
soul glaring at you as you are the most perfect
being they witnessed in their time of existence.
You don't see them counting your flaws, they
look at you like they could see all your flaws
and still chooses to appreciate them
Just like how we look up in the sky on starry
night and we feel lost and mesmerised by the
shine of the stars and the beauty of the moon
despite the darkness of the sky.

His touch on my skin felt like blooming fresh
cotton bud.
He pulled me closer, closer to his chest where I
could hear his heartbeat like a storm coming
near but I wasn't afraid.
I felt his breath on bare skin
It made me feel like I couldn't come this close to
anyone ever and this person next to me right
now has seen me, like there is nothing left to
hide.
He wrapped me around his arms like a blanket in
the first night of snow and in that same moment
it felt home.
He slid his hand touching my waist, I felt his
fingers slowly near my inner thigh but I looked
scared as a child in a new school on her first day.
He made assure that I was fine by asking me if I
was okay? my answer was "I don't know" which
confused him as much it did to me but the voice
inside me said how would you if it's okay if you
don't know what's okay?
The only thing I was sure of was that I felt safe
and certain that he wouldn't hurt me.
He kissed me on my forehead and he said to me
"it's going to hurt a little baby but the pleasure
of it makes you experience a little of more you,
it familiarises you more intensely with the
hidden versions and desires in you"

So it was a time of dawn, I felt my hymen
breaking as I moaned with the pleasure and pain
as I witnessed my first orgasm.
My body was covered in sweat from the warmth
of his body , his heart.
It made me meet a version of me, I never knew
existed.
I felt breathlessness, racing heartbeat, the
adrenaline rush and halt on my thoughts all at
once as I looked into his smile with a wrinkle on
his left cheek. Next day, it seemed like just
another normal with coffee in the morning and
wine in the evening but I felt different, I felt a
little more of me

Artist

I picked up my shattered pieces, all on my own
At my pace, one by one
Little did I know
It was a beginning of a master piece.

Unapologetically me

Its going to be hard
As I decide to prioritize myself
Say "NO" to things I don't wish to
ooh, that's sounds so liberating
little did I know
All I had to do to be happy was
Be unapologetically myself.

Let me be.

Let me feel for a minute that my size doesn't
matter
Let me feel that my colour be it fair, dark or
pale, It doesn't matter
Let me be me, just for a minute to look myself in
the mirror and not criticize my curves.
I need to shower my soul with love to heal my
scars
I need myself to be in love with what I see
Its not just my body, not just scars
Its the courage I carry,
its the smile I put on everyday,
its the kindness I spread.
So baby, when next time someone hands me
rose,
I won't doubt myself, I'll grab it in a moment
Because I am not good enough, I am more than
enough.

The Hypocrite lover

The love, we hear in the stories.

I hear these stories of love, bond and sacrifices but it's seems unrealistic to meet someone who makes you feel that the heartbreaks altogether wasn't that bad compared to how fucking good you make me feel when I just enter the same room as of you.

I hear these tales of people fantasying love stories which resembles to the one we see in movies, which starts on spill of coffee on the boy's white t-shirt and end on airport with kissing the girl and sometimes on a flash mob.

When I recall my memories of being in love, I remember falling so hard for him. I remember the silent music in the chaos, I remember him clearly walking towards me while the crowd was still blur and I remember the exact moment when I fell in love with him when he first smiled with first drop of rain in the early winter.

It was dreamy & confusing but the most purest feeling.

I couldn't resist my feelings even a little and all I
could remember was losing myself in the vision
of "us".

In loving his flaws, I overanalysed mine.
In fighting with him, I forgot my worth and in
supporting him unconditionally , I forgot
following my dreams.

And on a early winter evening, we part our ways
with love in our heart.
I knew It will be quiet
I knew there will be tears
I knew I will be standing alone
but I knew I am gonna be fine because I could
breathe a little more & dream a little freely.

Without any guilt of being selfish even when I
wasn't, without any hesitation to follow my
dreams. I choose a path, a path where I walked
alone to a journey of exploring myself in order
to value myself a little more and accept my true
self and my worth.

So the tales of love we hear are censored, they
are filtered with the ups and downs, mistakes,
flaws and hurtful decisions.

I feel like a hypocrite when I say that what I
believe in and what I want aren't the same.
But won't blame myself for that.
It's not my mistake that love doesn't seems
realistic to me anymore.
Or the red heart seems more dangerous sign than
the skull.

But what I want is that madness even if it
shatters my heart once again, I want that long
kiss which end on one of us smiling with bliss of
being in love. I want the love where when I look
into his eyes, I see this fear of losing me killing
him and the love between us keeping him alive.
I want that love which satisfies my soul and
makes me feel it worth the pain all over again.

I want the love
we hear, we see in movies but UNCENSORED
UNFILTERED .

Is it love?

Lying next to you
Your head resting upon my chest
I could hear you breathing,
Wishing you could sense my sadness or feel my
tears rolling down through my eyes in your hair .

Lying there next to you
I wonder if you ever loved me the way I love
you
The way you said you will,
But I find myself begging for that love
So when you show me a little love,
I cling on to it like a snow on a tree in winter
evening
It doesn't feel real anymore because all I get
from you , is all what I ask not what I deserve

Is that love?
It all just confuses me
I doubt, if it was ever about me
It was about you, you loved being loved by me
Love is consuming , that I was aware of
But not draining, filling you felt like filling a
broken glass.
It took all love I had within me and leaving you
empty too.

The unlearnt lesson

Let go of the idea, the image of you
To find the real you
Try all the things that excites you, seems a bit
new
That's life, it reforms you
At every stage, you feel you have yourself
And an unlearnt lesson hits your way
It's a pattern of universe
It teaches you, makes you aware
So if next time you feel you are lost
Hold on tight, you are on the right path with just
a little extra homework

A Letter to myself

To my 15 year old me,
I am here fulfilling all dreams you dreamt.
I wish I could tell you how proud your parents
are today.
I know they don't express in words.
but their eyes shine
They shine as they see you making your life on
your own
Its just not your degrees or money you make,
you are more than that.
You are going to travel all places you wanted to
But oh please, believe in yourself
Hold on tight
Do not give up on the stupid ideas,
because just with a little patience
You will be there.
Leaving your bullies, enemies and bad parts
behind.
For a future, you will build
I request you to forgive them, forgive yourself
Don't burden yourself with the insecurities they
gave you
Don't carry the traumas they scarred you with
They don't define you.
You my little, you are more than that.

The Answer

The key to your happiness relies within you,
The answer might me known by a few.
It sounds easy but hard to do,
The truest form of happiness is allowing
yourself to be just you
even if all the eyes are on you.

Adulting Alarm

19

As I grew up
My priorities changed.
Now I find calmness in the first cup of tea in
morning.
I find joy in my hustling work,
I find peace watching the sky's colours change
as the sun sets
Adulthood might sounds alarming or look
frightening but you get used to it in your own
way.
You build these boundaries to protect yourself,
You pickup best habits to nourish yourself,
You choose your inner circle wisely,
Before you realise you become so content to
yourself.
That making yourself happy becomes your sole
responsibility.

PS

Feel her, her warmth
Her lips, against yours
Make her smile,
With a gentle nuzzle.
She is extraordinary, worth all the pain.
So just,
Hold her tight
All day, all night.

PS

21

Holding hands
Silence between them
Interrupted by his racing heartbeats,
As she was the most beautiful girl he ever met.

PS

Why did you stopped writing?
They asked me.
I couldn't answer
As I got lost in the thought
Why?
And a tear rolled down on my cheek
Maybe I was scared,
I was scared what might come out on to pages
which I am hiding even from myself.
My pain felt stronger
Full of rage, disappointment & grief that I was
filled with
I was scared that as I would begin to write, I
might burst into tears and no one would be there
as I fall apart.
But isn't it normal to be scared to fall apart
right?
But if someone ask me today, why did you
stopped writing?
I would say" I was stupid"
I would grab my pen right away.
And write till my heart burst all of the pain, pass
it down to the fresh white pages of my diary till
ink runs out or my tears.
As I am on my healing journey

And healing myself shouldn't be something I
should be scared of.

PS

24

Its okay to be hurt.
Who isn't?

The After

Standing still on the door
I saw him leaving just for another normal day,
but my heart felt an ache knowing its the last
time I would kiss him, its the last time I would
hug him and take a breath in his arms.
Its not about meeting again, its about the way I
wanted him at that moment won't be same as I
decide to move forward on my pace.
He was all I ever dreamt of and turned into all I
never wanted even in my nightmares.
You scarred me

I often find myself, finding this closure which I
can't get from you because for you its just the
story that ended when I left .
But for me
There was a after and a before.

My beloved Grandmother (Dadi)

She was my roommate
my cheerleader, my critic, my teacher
She taught me to be love selflessly,
She taught me how to be kind,
She was my constant source of happiness.

Pushed me towards my dreams
She was my light on dark nights,
She believed in me like no one else did,
She was my person.

I remember her waiting for me as I come from
school,
I remember her being proud when I got into
college,
i remember her having tears in her eyes as I left
home for university.

But when she left
there was this void and unimaginable pain
Words and tears couldn't do justice to what I felt
She left knowing I loved her tremendously.
Never did she let any opportunity pass by to let
me know how she felt for me

I feel her presence in my bad times,
And blessings in my good times.
Undoubtedly, she is being missed but maybe she
wanted to make the sky shine brighter with her
presence.
I miss you dadi.
- Your fan :)